The Complete .NET Video Course

BERTRAND MEYER

President and CTO
Interactive Software Engineering,
Santa Barbara (CA)

Professor (adjunct)
Monash University,
Melbourne (Australia)

Prentice Hall PTR
Upper Saddle River, New Jersey 07458

Plan

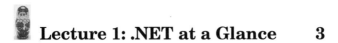

Check these Web sites!

http://www.dotnetexperts.com

.   • NET info, public seminars, discussion group...

http://www.dotnetexperts.com/ptrcourse

   • Supplementary material for this course

http://www.eiffel.com

   • ISE and Eiffel home page, lots of O-O material

http://www.tools-conferences.com

   • The TOOLS conferences home page

PART A

OVERVIEW

Lecture 1

.NET at a Glance

Famous last words . . .

" . . . a ton of vaporware that even Microsoft does not expect to ship for years . . ."

Bob Metcalfe
InfoWorld
July 2000

Notes:

_____

_____

_____

_____

_____

_____

Timeline

- 1991: Windows 3.1
- 1995: Microsoft Embraces the Internet
- 1996: MS Embraces Java—Visual J++
- October 1997: Sun Sues MS Over Java
- 1997/1998: Start of .NET Project
- 1999: Inclusion of External Partners
- July 2000: .NET Announced
- October 2000: First Public Beta
- Mid-2001 (?): First Public Release

Notes:

_____

_____

_____

_____

_____

_____

ISE/Monash timeline

- Contacts in April 1999
- Aim of Collaboration: To Port Eiffel Implementation
- Work started September 1999
- First Delivery for Microsoft Professional Development Conference, July 2000
- Key Personnel: Raphael Simon and Emmanuel Stapf (ISE), Christine Mingins (Monash)

Notes:

_____

_____

_____

_____

_____

_____

PDC 2000

What is .NET? (NOT)

- Not an operating system
- Not a programming language
- Not an interface definition language

Notes:

_____

_____

_____

_____

_____

_____

What is .NET? (NOT)

- Not an operating system
                        (yet)
- Not a programming language
- Not an interface definition language

Notes:

_____

_____

_____

_____

_____

_____

What is .NET?

- A language-neutral platform for enterprise and Web development

Notes:

_____

_____

_____

_____

_____

In plain English, please . . .

- A virtual machine above the operating system
- A language interoperability architecture
- A common runtime for many languages
- An architecture for Internet and Web development
- A component model, replacing COM
- A standardized versioning mechanism
- A uniform security policy
- Thousands of reusable components
- An interoperability standard: SOAP
- The cornerstone of Microsoft's future developments

Notes:

_____

_____

_____

_____

_____

Problems addressed

- Single model for Web and non-Web (e.g., client-server) development
- Web services
- Easy deployment of applications
- Application versioning
- Application security
- Application independence
- Dealing with many languages
- Component combination with lean interfaces

Notes:

_____

_____

_____

_____

_____

_____

Some immediate practical consequences

- End of "DLL Hell"
- "Smart Web sites"
- Multi-language development, including multi-language inheritance, debugging . . .
- No more IDL
- Strong security mechanisms
- Standard database interface: ADO+
- Scalability: from PDA to Web farm

Notes:

_____

_____

_____

_____

_____

_____

For COM developers:

Many familiar concepts (e.g., interfaces); well-mapped transition path; but:

- No more IDL
- No more MIDL compiler, ATL . . .
- No more AddRef, Release, QueryInterface
- No more IUnknown, IDispatch, . . .
- No more GUIDs
- No more type libraries
- No more HRESULT
- Wider use of inheritance

Notes:

_____

_____

_____

_____

_____

_____

Lecture 2

A First Demo

Demo 1: A .NET Medley

Some of what you'll see in this demo:

- ASP+ (Active Server Pages +)
- Combining presentation with processing
- Our first C# example
- Eiffel on .NET
- Multi-language combination
- Server-side mechanisms, server controls

Notes:

_____

_____

_____

_____

_____

TOOLS USA registration

(from: http://dotnet.eiffel.com)

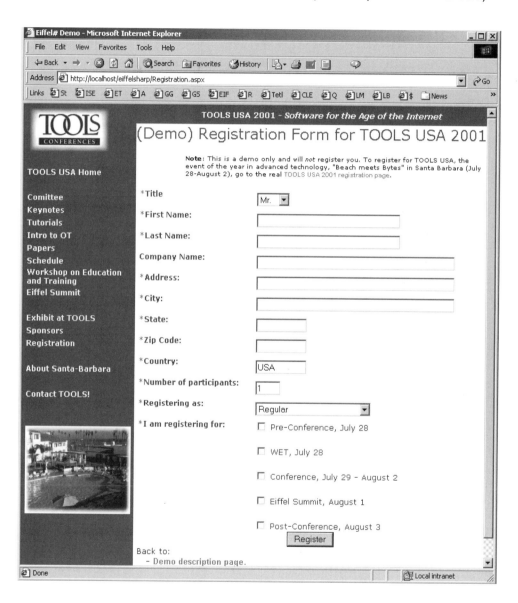

(See live demo)

What's in a binary?

- ... Not your grandmother's .exe!
- ... Not your grandfather's .dll!

Notes:

_____

_____

_____

_____

_____

_____

PART B

THE CHALLENGES
(IF .NET IS THE ANSWER, WHAT IS THE QUESTION?)

 Lecture 3: The Internet and the Web

 Lecture 4: Object Technology

 Lecture 5: Component Technology

Lecture 3

The Internet
and the Web

The Internet and the Web

- Ubiquitous
- Not just computers: Internet appliances
- WAP, WML

Notes:

_____

_____

_____

_____

_____

_____

Web page, ca. 1994

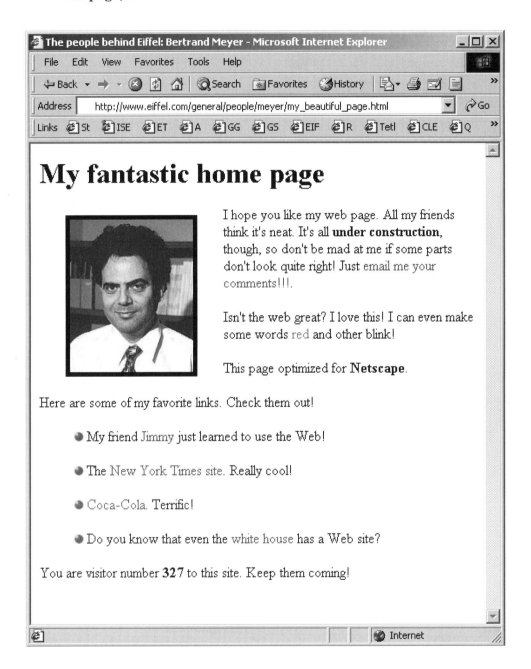

Web page, ca. 1996

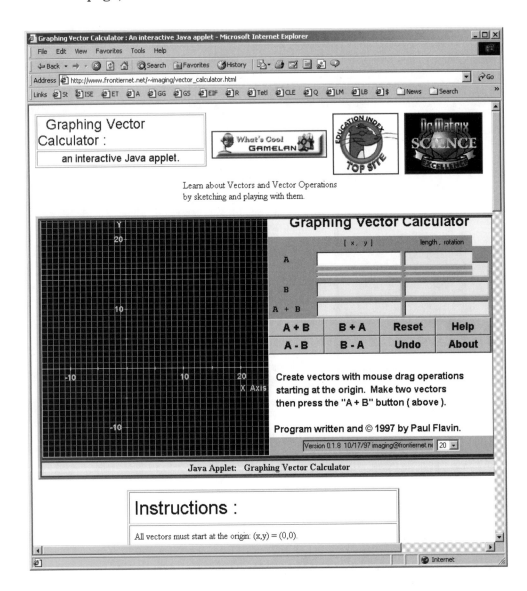

Web page, ca. 1998

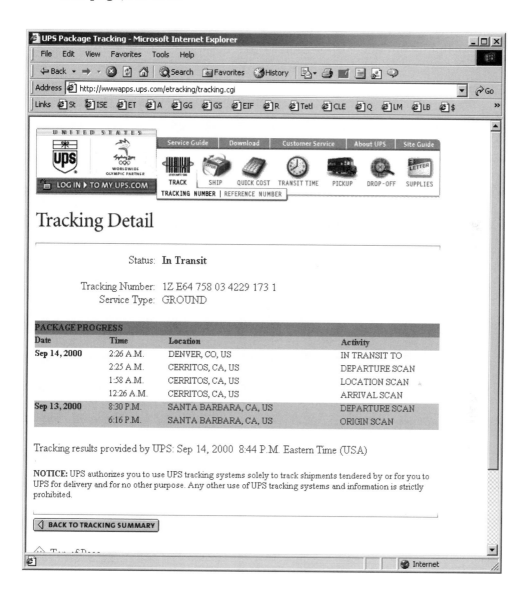

The Web and the Business

- No longer marketing brochures
- Bringing out the corporation's business model, for everyone to see

Notes:

_____

_____

_____

_____

_____

Towards "smart" web pages

Client side:

- Javascript, Dynamic HTML . . .

Server side:

- CGI scripts
- ASP (Microsoft's Active Server Pages)
- JSP (Java Server Pages)

Notes:

_____

_____

_____

_____

_____

_____

The Web: it's not just for browsing

Web services:

- Make the capabilities of a Web page available to programs

Building Block Services:

- Make the capabilities of a Web page available to other Web pages

Examples:

- Authentication
- User preferences
- Stocks, news, . . .
- Time, calendar, . . .

Notes:

_____

_____

_____

_____

_____

_____

But what about security?

If we are bringing the business model out . . .

- Reliability and availability critical
  - Frequent disasters
  - Common problems: memory leaks, unhandled errors, unexpected crashes
- Not only email and viruses
- ActiveX controls
- Buffer overflow technique

Notes:

_____

_____

_____

_____

_____

_____

The buffer overflow technique

- Find a program that puts it argument into a finite-size buffer and doesn't check that the argument fits
- Use a big enough argument to overflow
- Find the place on the execution stack where the return address is stored; include it in the argument
- Also include your own program . . .
- Step-by-step recipes on the Web

Notes:

_____

_____

_____

_____

_____

_____

Overflowing a buffer

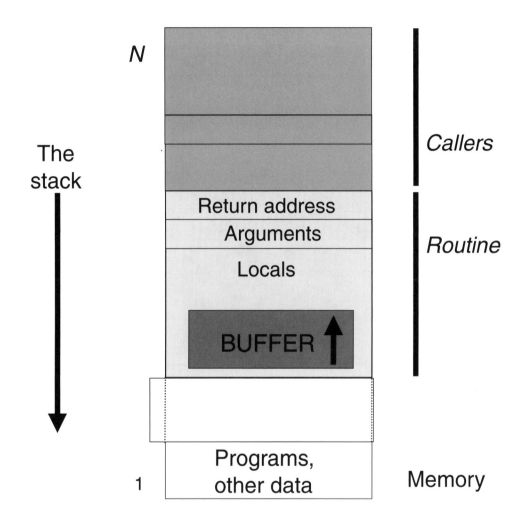

Overflowing a buffer

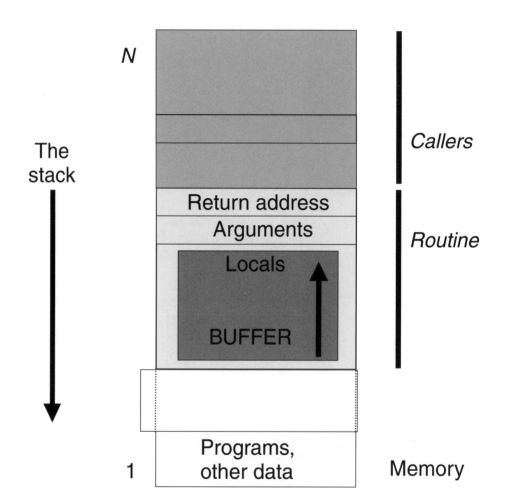

Overflowing a buffer

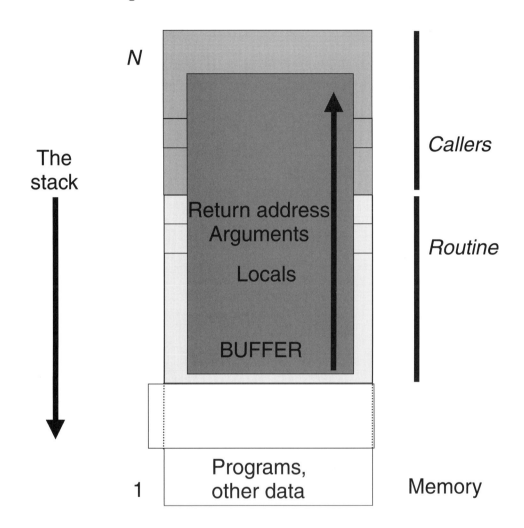

Lessons from the buffer overflow problem

- Lack of typing: things can pretend to be something else than what they are
- Simplistic notion of security: all or nothing
- Lack of Design by Contract: no specification of expected properties

Notes:

_____

_____

_____

_____

_____

_____

Lecture 4

Object Technology

Behind .NET: object technology

- Emphasis: modular, decentralized architectures
- Class: module based on an abstractly defined type of data
- Information hiding, data abstraction
- Inheritance, polymorphism, dynamic binding

Notes:

_____

_____

_____

_____

_____

_____

Information hiding

Access every object through the official operations ("features") of its interface

- Example: WINDOW object. Features:
  - height, width, border_color
  - add_button, resize, change_border_color . . .
- Some features are "queries", others are "commands"

Notes:

_____

_____

_____

_____

_____

Information hiding violations (e.g., C++, Java)

- Direct field modification:

```
x.some_field := some_value
```

- O-O form:

```
x.set_field (some_value)

        set_field (v: TYPE) is
            do
                    field := v
            end
```

Notes:

_____

_____

_____

_____

_____

_____

System structure

Two relations between classes:

- Client: "uses" relation; goes through interface; information hiding
- Inheritance: "extends" or "specializes" relation; doesn't necessarily go through interface

Notes:

_____

_____

_____

_____

_____

_____

Inheritance: organize abstractions into hierarchies

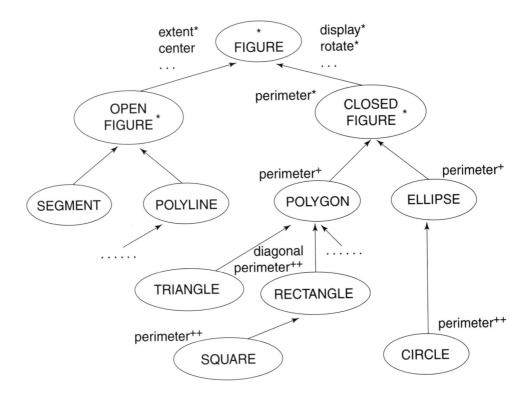

Notes:

_____

_____

_____

_____

_____

_____

Inheritance concepts

- Redefinition
- Polymorphism
- Dynamic binding
- Deferred (or "abstract") features and classes

Notes:

_____

_____

_____

_____

_____

_____

More O-O techniques

- Multiple inheritance
- Genericity
- Design by Contract™

Notes:

_____

_____

_____

_____

_____

_____

Multiple inheritance

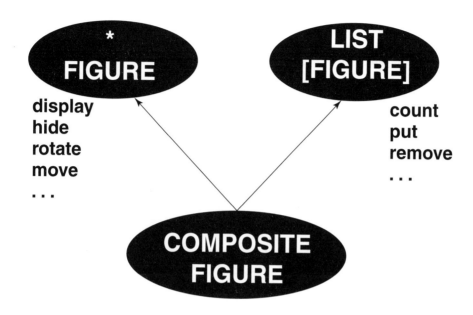

Notes:

_____

_____

_____

_____

_____

_____

Multiple inheritance

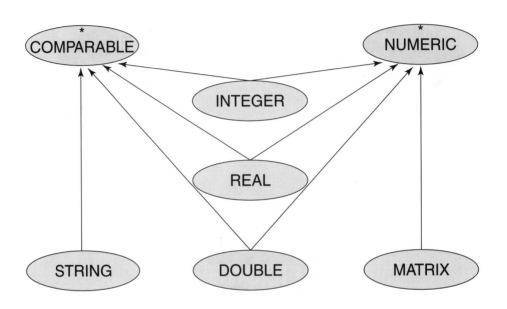

Notes:

_____

_____

_____

_____

_____

_____

Multiple inheritance from interfaces: limitations

- It is often useful to have a mix of abstract and concrete ("effective") features
- Eiffel "deferred" classes permit this
- Not possible in Java and the .NET object model
- Java experience shows that programmers resort to various ugly tricks to simulate this . . .(See John Viega, TOOLS USA 2000)

Notes:

Multiple inheritance

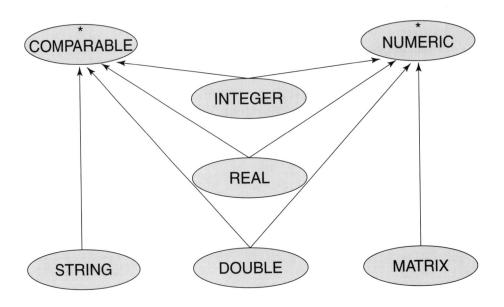

Notes:

_____

_____

_____

_____

_____

_____

deferred class COMPARABLE [G] **feature**

```
infix "<" (other: COMPARABLE [G]: Boolean is
    deferred
    end
```

```
infix "<=" (other: COMPARABLE [G]: Boolean is
    do
        Result:= Current < other or
            equal (Current, other)
    end
```

```
infix ">=" (other: COMPARABLE [G] is ...
infix "<" (other: COMPARABLE [G] is ...
...
```

end -- class COMPARABLE

Notes:

_____

_____

_____

_____

_____

_____

Genericity

```
class LIST [G] feature
        put (x: G; i: INTEGER) is …
        entry (i: INTEGER) : G
        …
end

employees: LIST [EMPLOYEE]
…
employees.put (Julia, 3)
…
print (employees.entry (3).salary)
```

Notes:

_____

_____

_____

_____

_____

_____

If no genericity

Run-time type checks: ("Assignment attempt" in Eiffel, "dynamic casts" or "type narrowing" in C++/Java)

```
x := employees.entry (3)
if "x is indeed an EMPLOYEE" then
      print (x.salary)
end
```

Notes:

_____

_____

_____

_____

_____

_____

Design By Contract™

- A method for building reliable software
- Based on metaphor of business contracts
- Basic ideas applicable to all languages
- Built-in into Eiffel language and tools

Notes:

_____

_____

_____

_____

_____

_____

```
class MY_WEB_PAGE inherit
        GENERIC_WEB_PAGE
feature
   refresh is
           -- Refresh the page
        require
           valid_connection: connection.open
        do
           if changed then update end
        ensure
           refreshed: old changed implies updated
        end
  ...
   changed: BOOLEAN
 invariant
   valid_connection: connection/=Void
end --   class MY_WEB_PAGE
```

Precondition

Postcondition

Class invariant

Notes:

_____

_____

_____

_____

_____

_____

Design By Contract: Applications

- Automatic, built-in documentation
- More systematic debugging process
- Serves as basis for tests
- Guides software construction process
- Helps requirements analysis
- Management tool

Notes:

_____

_____

_____

_____

_____

_____

Lecture 5

Component Technology

O-O communication standards

Common aim:

Let applications cooperate on the basis of O-O principles

Notes:

_____

_____

_____

_____

_____

_____

An executable application

Notes:

_____

_____

_____

_____

_____

_____

An application with plugs

Notes:

_____

_____

_____

_____

_____

_____

Interconnection models

- CORBA (Object Management Group)
- J2EE (Java 2 Platform Enterprise Edition) with Enterprise Java Beans (Sun)
- COM (Microsoft)

Notes:

_____

_____

_____

_____

_____

Interconnection models

- One language, many platforms
- One platform, several languages
- Many platforms, many languages

Notes:

_____

_____

_____

_____

_____

_____

Interconnection models

- One language, many platforms
  - J2EE
- One platform, several languages
  - COM
- Many platforms, many languages
  - CORBA

Notes:

_____

_____

_____

_____

_____

_____

CORBA

- Multi-language standard
- CORBA 1 (1991), CORBA 2 (1996), CORBA 3 (1999)
- IIOP (Internet Inter-Orb Protocol): the universal mechanism for client-server communication
- Module description: through IDL (Interface Description Language)

Notes:

_____

_____

_____

_____

_____

CORBA architecture

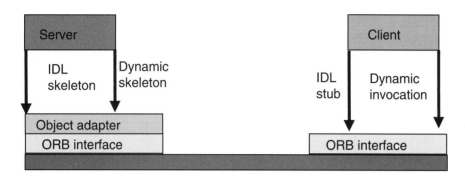

Notes:

_____

_____

_____

_____

_____

_____

CORBA IDL example

```
module Flight_reservations
  {interface Bookings {
    exception Invalid_seat {SEAT where;};
    exception Already_booked {SEAT where;};
    exception Not_booked {SEAT where;};
    readonly attribute string name;
    readonly attribute unsigned short row_count;
    readonly attribute unsigned short seats_per_row;
  {short free_seat_count ();
  SEATS available_seats ();
  PRICE get_price (in SEATS requested_seats)
        raises (Invalid_seat);
  boolean make_booking (in SEATS requested)
        raises (Invalid_seat, Already_booked);
  boolean cancel_booking (in SEATS requested)
        raises (Invalid_seat, Not_booked);
  };
}
```

Notes:

_____

_____

_____

_____

_____

_____

Java and J2EE / Java Beans

Java as a programming language

- Simplified version of C++
- More O-O, but retains close connection to C
- Designed for garbage collection
- Single inheritance (multiple for "interfaces")
- Virtual machine: JVM, for interpretation of portable Java "bytecode" or compilation
- Dynamic class loading

Notes:

_____

_____

_____

_____

_____

_____

Enterprise Java Beans

- A standard for communicating components using the Java technology and the Java language
- Event-driven model: listeners and notifiers
- Introspection mechanisms: enable a client to ask a bean about available facilities
- Java Server Pages (JSP)

Notes:

_____

_____

_____

_____

_____

_____

Enterprise Java Beans

- Session Beans: frontline to clients
  - Stateful
  - Stateless
- Entity Beans: encapsulation of server data
  - Bean-managed persistence: take care of data manipulation operations
  - Container-managed persistence: leave them to container

Notes:

_____

_____

_____

_____

_____

_____

EJB 3-tier tools

- Remote Method Interface
- CORBA IDL interfaces
- JDBC: database interface
- JTS/JTA: transaction server interface
- JNDI: directory services
- AWT, Swing: GUI libraries
- . . .

Notes:

_____

_____

_____

_____

_____

_____

COM

- Until .NET, principal component model on Windows
- Evolution of earlier Microsoft technologies
- Binary component model

Notes:

_____

_____

_____

_____

_____

_____

COM history

- Clipboard (Macintosh, Windows . . .): copy-paste
- DDE (Dynamic Data Exchange): import, by reference, elements from one document into another, e.g., Word and spreadsheet
- OLE 1 (1990): composite documents; include by reference ("linking") or value ("embedding")
- OLE 2 : In-place editing
- COM: Abstract object interfaces
- Active elements: ActiveX (cf. JavaBeans)

Notes:

_____

_____

_____

_____

_____

_____

The COM model

- Every component has a unique identifier (GUID) determined by statistical algorithm.
- Every component provides a set of interfaces; every interface is a set of functionalities.
- Some operations supported by every component
  (from IUnknown interface):
  - QueryInterface
  - AddRef
  - Release

Notes:

_____

_____

_____

_____

_____

_____

COM double indirection

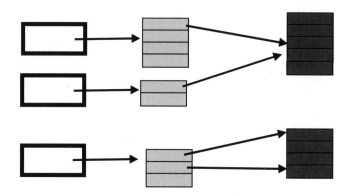

Notes:

_____

_____

_____

_____

_____

_____

COM registration

- Before being used, a COM component must be registered
- Uses a central registry

Notes:

_____

_____

_____

_____

_____

_____

COM IDL

```
[ object,
   uuid(45Df3F4B0-DB76-11d1-AA06-0040052510F1)
]
interface IComputeSalesTax : IUnknown
{
import "unknwn.idl"
   HRESULT Calculate
           ([in] long Sales_amount,
            [in] long Origin_zip_code,
            [in] long Destination_zip_code,
            [out, retval] long* Sales_tax
}
```

Notes:

_____

_____

_____

_____

_____

_____

COM inheritance

- Applies to interfaces
- Not connected to polymorphism
- In practice, tends to be used mostly for inheriting from system-defined interfaces

Notes:

_____

_____

_____

_____

_____

_____

The IDispatch interface

Provides one more level of abstraction: use the method name as argument; reflection mechanism.

Four methods:
- GetTypeInfoCount
- GetTypeInfo
- GetIdsOfNames
- Invoke

A method can have a regular interface as well as be available through IDispatch.

Notes:

_____

_____

_____

_____

_____

COM versioning

- Once published and given a GUID, a COM interface may not be changed.
- "Versioning" is provided by moving to a different interface.

Notes:

_____

_____

_____

_____

_____

_____

COM and distribution

- DCOM: version of COM allowing clients and servers to run on different machines.
- "Marshalling" of values between components
- .NET suggests migration to XML- and HTTP-based techniques.

Notes:

_____

_____

_____

_____

_____

_____

Component-based development

- Szyperski (*Component Software*, Addison-Wesley, 1998):
  - "Binary unit of independent production, acquisition, and deployment that interacts to form a functioning system."
- Characteristic properties:
  - Unit of independent deployment
  - Unit of third-party composition
  - No persistent state

Notes:

_____

_____

_____

_____

_____

_____

Why binary?

- The real issue: information hiding

See "Software development" columns since November 1999.

Notes:

Information hiding violations

- Direct field modification:
```
x.some_field := some_value
```
- O-O form:
```
x.set_field (some_value)

set_field (v: TYPE) is
        do
                field := v
        end
```

Notes:

_____

_____

_____

_____

_____

_____

A more general definition

A component is a program element with the following three properties:

- It may be used by other program elements (as opposed to just humans, or non-software systems). These elements are called its "clients".
- The component's authors need not know about the clients.
- The clients' authors need only know what the component's authors have decided to tell them.

Notes:

_____

_____

_____

_____

_____

_____

Issues with CBD models

- Language independence
- Common conceptual model
- IDL (see next)
- Ease of component construction and deployment: heavy interface work
- Component quality
- How do we know that a component will do its job?

Notes:

_____

_____

_____

_____

_____

_____

Interoperability issues

- Hard to combine languages
- Call-out facilities
- Subtle differences in basic data types (what is an integer?)
- Differences in object models
- Can you inherit from my class?

Notes:

_____

_____

_____

_____

_____

_____

IDL limitations

- IDL compilers go the wrong way! (Some tools correct this, e.g., ATL, CORBA decompilers, EiffelCOM Wizard)
- Need to write IDL spec
- Imperfect object model

Notes:

_____

_____

_____

_____

_____

_____

The self-documentation principle

> ### Documentation is something
> ### that computers do

- Example: Eiffel "contract form"
- Reconstruct interface from code
- Tools will produce views of the system in various forms and at various levels of abstraction

Notes:

_____

_____

_____

_____

_____

_____

Example: EiffelCOM wizard

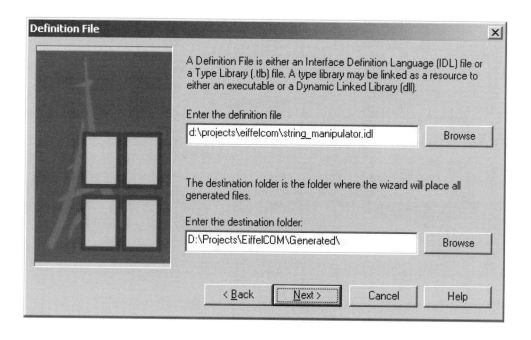

Notes:

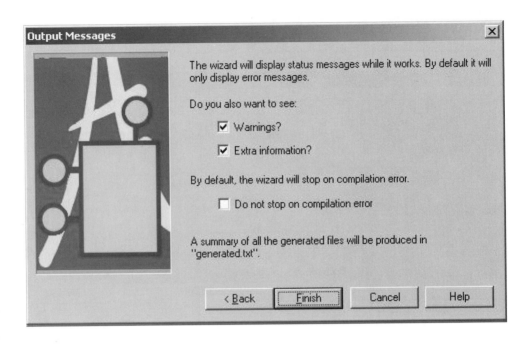

Notes:

_____

_____

_____

_____

_____

_____

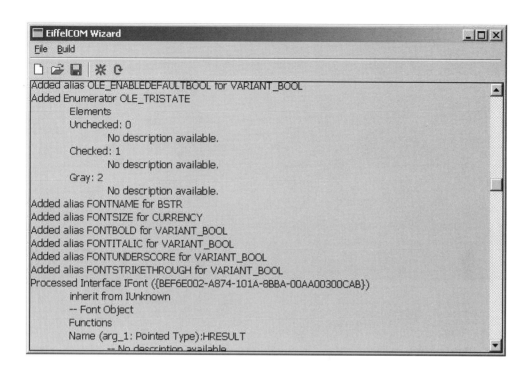

Notes:

_____

_____

_____

_____

_____

_____

PART C

THE PRODUCTS

 Lecture 6: What products are affected?

 Lecture 7: A survey of the libraries

 Lecture 8: Frameworks: ASP+, ADO+, Win Forms, Web Forms, . . .

Lecture 6

What products are affected?

The .NET architecture

.NET Platform

Interchange standards

Frameworks

Runtime

VOS

Notes:

_____

_____

_____

_____

_____

The .NET platform

Notes:

_____

_____

_____

_____

_____

.NET scope

A general platform for future Microsoft products. Already announced:

- Host Integration Server 2000
- SQL Server 2000
- Biztalk Server 2000
- Visual Studio .NET
- Application Center 2000
- Commerce Server 2000
- Exchange Server 2000
- Internet Security and Acceleration Server 2000

Notes:

_____

_____

_____

_____

_____

_____

Towards a common development environment

- Visual Studio.NET
- Common API
- Common back end, editing, browsing, debugging tools
- Currently or in progress: Microsoft languages, COBOL, Eiffel, APL, . . .

Notes:

Interchange standards

XML, SOAP, persistence . . .

Notes:

_____

_____

_____

_____

_____

XML

Standard format for exchanging data:

- Text-based (Unicode)
- Structured, arbitrary depth
- Self-describing

Present throughout the .NET architecture as the mechanism of choice to exchange data and define configuration settings

Notes:

_____

_____

_____

_____

_____

_____

SOAP

- Simple Object Access Protocol
- Defined by Microsoft, IBM, others
- XML format for exchanging objects (as in OOP)

Notes:

_____

_____

_____

_____

_____

_____

SOAP example

```
<SOAP-ENV:Envelope>
    <SOAP-ENV:Body>

 <xmlns:m="http://www.scores.com/baseball"/>
        <m:GetScore>
        <TeamName>Pioneers</TeamName>
        </m:GetScore>
    </SOAP-ENV:Body>
</SOAP-ENV:Envelope>
```

Notes:

_____

_____

_____

_____

_____

_____

Lecture 7

A survey of the libraries

Library examples

System	Basic types: Object, Byte, Char, Array, Int32, Exception, String . . .
System.Collections	Collection types: ArrayList, BitArray, Dictionary, Hashtable, Queue, SortedList, Stack . . .
System.Globalization	Internationalization: Calendar, NumberFormatInfo, RegionInfo . . .
System.Net	Network communication: WebRequest, WebResponse, TcpClient, TcpListener, UdpClient, Sockets
System.Reflection	Inspection of metadata: Assembly, ConstructorInfo, FieldInfo, MemberInfo, MethodInfo, Module, ParameterInfo . . .
System.Security	Security Features: Permissions, Policy, Principal, Util, Cryptography . . .
System.Web.UI. WebControls	Graphical controls for Web-based applications: AdRotator, BorderStyle, Data Grid, HyperLink, ListBox, Panel, RadioButton, Table . . .
System.WinForms	Graphical controls: Button, CheckBox, DataGrid, FileDialog, Form, ListBox, MainMenu, MonthCalendar, RichEdit, ToolBarTreeView . . .
System.Data	Relational database management: DataBinding, DataRelation, DataRow, DataSet, DataTable
System.Drawing. Design	Design-time user interface and drawing support: BitmapEditor, DrawingToolboxItem, FontEditor, UIType Editor
System.Runtime. InteropServices	COM interoperability

Notes:

_____

_____

_____

_____

_____

More libraries

- System.Runtime.Serialization
- System.Runtime.Serialization.Formatters
- System.Runtime.Serialization.Formatters.Binary
- System.Security.Cryptography
- System.Security.Permissions
- System.Security.Policy
- System.Security.Principal

Notes:

_____

_____

_____

_____

_____

_____

More libraries

- System.ServiceProcess
- System.Text
- System.Text.RegularExpressions
- System.Threading
- System.Timers

Notes:

_____

_____

_____

_____

_____

_____

Libraries

- System.Web
- System.Web.Caching
- System.Web.Configuration
- System.Web.Security
- System.Web.Services.Description
- System.Web.Services.Discovery
- System.Web.Services.Protocols

Notes:

_____

_____

_____

_____

_____

_____

Libraries

- System.Xml
- System.Xml.Serialize
- System.Xml.Xpath
- System.Xml.Xsl

Notes:

_____

_____

_____

_____

_____

_____

Lecture 8

Frameworks: ASP+, ADO+, Win Forms, Web Forms, ...

The frameworks

Notes:

_____

_____

_____

_____

_____

_____

ASP+ (Active Server Pages +)

- Web development platform
- Combine or separate code and content
- Integrated with .NET languages and the rest of an enterprise's software base
- Compiled
- Caching: compiled pages are kept until not needed, or changed.
- Live update of applications: no need to shut down server

Notes:

_____

_____

_____

_____

_____

_____

An ASP+ page

(from: http://dotnet.eiffel.com)

```
Registration.aspx - Notepad                                                    _□ x
File Edit Format Help
<%@ Assembly Name="registrationservice" %>
<%@ Import Namespace="RegistrationService" %>
<%@ Page Language="C#" %>

<HTML>
        <HEAD>
               <META HTTP-EQUIV="Content-TyPe" CONTENT="text/html; charset=windows-1252">
               <TITLE>Eiffel# Demo</TITLE>
               <LINK REL="stylesheet" TYPE="text/css" HREF="usa.css">
               <LINK HREF="http://www.eiffel.com/images/interface/eiffel_purple.ico" REL="SHORTCUT ICON">
               <SCRIPT RUNAT="SERVER">

                       bool registered, register_click;
                       String error_message;
                       Registrar registrar;

                       void Page_Init( Object Source, EventArgs E )
                       {
                               registrar = new Registrar();
                               registrar.start();
                               Application ["Registrar"] = registrar;
                               registered = false;
                               register_click = false;
                       }

                       void Register_Click( Object Source, EventArgs E )
                       {
                               register_click = true;

                               // Add registrant
                               registrar.add_registrant( address_form.SelectedItem.Value,
                                                          first_name.Value,
                                                          last_name.Value,
                                                          company_name.Value,
                                                          address.Value,
```

Notes:

_____

_____

_____

_____

_____

_____

Web forms

- Programmable Web pages, using ASP+
- Numerous tools available, including Visual Studio.NET
- Rich set of controls
- Object model; event model
- Scalable, not dependent on performance of client computer or other device
- Rich set of controls, beyond HTML
- Adapts to browser: generates HTML, dynamic HTML, . . .

Notes:

Web form example

(source: MSDN)

1. Select HTML controls from the Toolbox

2. Drag controls to the HTML designer

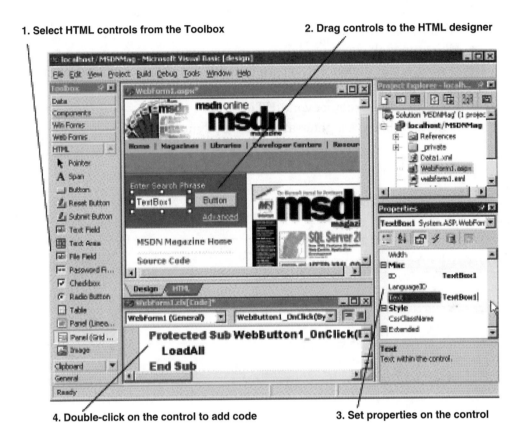

4. Double-click on the control to add code

3. Set properties on the control

Notes:

_____

_____

_____

_____

ASP+ server controls

- Intrinsic controls
  - Button, ImageButton
  - TextBox, CheckBox, RadioButton
  - DropDownList, ListBox
  - Table, TableRow, TableCell
- List controls
  - Repeater, DataList, DataGrid
- "Rich" controls
  - Calendar, AdRotator, . . .
- Validation controls
  - RangeValidator, RegularExpressionValidator, RequiredFieldValidator, CustomValidator . . .

Notes:

_____

_____

_____

_____

_____

_____

Session management

- Identify requests from a single browser as constituting a single session
- Management events: OnSessionStart, OnSessionEnd
- Manage application state: synchronization of concurrent access to global variables; protection from other applications

Notes:

_____

_____

_____

_____

_____

_____

ASP+ configuration

- Stored in XML files
- Extendible
- Changes automatically detected
- Examples:
  - Localization
  - Security
  - Needed assemblies

Notes:

_____

_____

_____

_____

_____

_____

ASP+ vs. ASP

- Compiled
- State and session management
- Server-side controls
- Better separation of code and content
- Full object model
- Open to any language
- Configuration, security, . . .
- Web services
- Direct connection with databases (ADO+)
- Browser-dependent rendering

Notes:

_____

_____

_____

_____

_____

_____

Web services

- Make all the capabilities of a Web server available as an API
- In .NET, it's already an API! (a set of types in an assembly)
- Glue is SOAP
- SDL: Services Description Language; SCL: SOAP Contract Language. XML formats enabling a Web site to advertise its services
- DISCO: Discovery protocol
- Yielding to WSDL: Web Services Description Language

Notes:

_____

_____

_____

_____

_____

_____

Web services

- In principle, do not require special protocol, like e.g., RMI (Java), DCOM: all is based on XML messages exchanged through HTTP
- In practice, of course, the structure must be understood the same way on both sides.

Notes:

_____

_____

_____

_____

_____

_____

Beyond Web services

- Building Block Services:
  - Web services from a Web site to a Web site.
- Examples:
  - Authentication
  - User preferences
  - Credit card info
  - Time and date
  - News, stocks, . . .

Notes:

_____

_____

_____

_____

_____

_____

Web Services Description Language (WSDL)

- Joint Microsoft-IBM development
- Published September 2000
- Replaces DISCO, SCL, . . .
- Mechanism for Web sites to advertise their services

Notes:

_____

_____

_____

_____

_____

WSDL

- Types: type definition to describe messages.
- Message: abstract definition of data being transmitted. Each part has type.
- Port Type: set of abstract operations referring to input and output messages.
- Binding: concrete protocol and data format for operations and messages of a Port Type.
- Port: address for a binding; defines single communication endpoint.
- Service: aggregates a set of related ports.

Notes:

_____

_____

_____

_____

_____

Databases: ADO+

- The successor to ODBC, OLE-DB and ADO
- Standard API to SQL databases
- For distributed applications, XML to exchange data between programs and Web pages (ADO/COM: marshalling); goes through firewalls
- Supports "DataSets": memory-resident relational database; populated by program or from database (ADO disconnected RecordSet)
- Managed provider: interface between database and DataSet

Notes:

_____

_____

_____

_____

_____

_____

Win Forms

- Encapsulates the native Win32 client-side API
- Simpler and cleaner than native API or MFC (Microsoft Foundation Classes, C++)
- Uses events and delegates instead of Windows message processing loop
- Win Form application derives from System.WinForms.Form and executes its "Run" method

Notes:

_____

_____

_____

_____

_____

_____

Setting an event handler (C#, using Win Forms)

```
clickme = new Button();
clickme.Text = "Click me!";
clickme.Location = new System.Drawing.Point (200, 30);
clickme.Size = new System.Drawing.Size (65, 65);

EventHandler my_handler = new EventHandler (action);
clickme.Click += my_handler;
```

Notes:

_____

_____

_____

_____

_____

_____

PART D

HOW IT WORKS

Lecture 9

.NET architecture

.NET components

- Common language runtime
- Component libraries
- Frameworks
- Interoperability standards

Notes:

_____

_____

_____

_____

_____

_____

.NET architecture

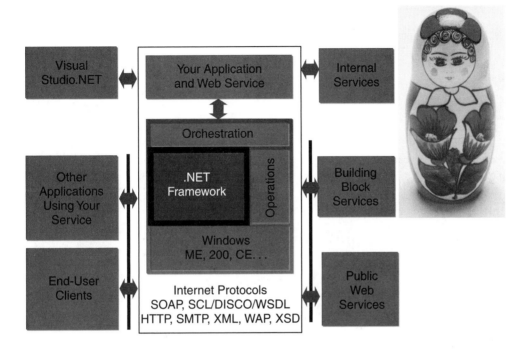

Notes:

_____

_____

_____

_____

_____

_____

The .NET framework

Web Services
Interchange, persistence
Reusable components
Common Language Runtime

Notes:

_____

_____

_____

_____

_____

_____

The .NET framework

Web Services	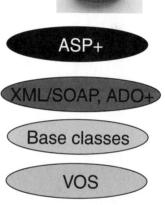 ASP+
Interchange, persistence	XML/SOAP, ADO+
Reusable components	Base classes
Common Language Runtime	VOS

Notes:

_____

_____

_____

_____

_____

Lecture 10

The Runtime

The Common Language Runtime

Notes:

_____

_____

_____

_____

_____

_____

The Common Language Runtime

- Basic set of mechanisms to execute .NET programs
- Virtual machine based on internal code: MSIL (Microsoft Intermediate Language)
- MSIL is not meant to be interpreted but "jitted" (Just-In-Time compiled) to native platform
- Built-in security mechanisms

Notes:

_____

_____

_____

_____

_____

_____

Execution model

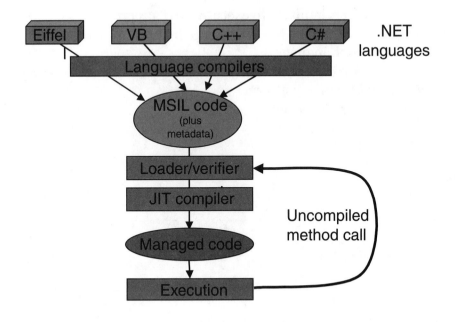

Notes:

_____

_____

_____

_____

_____

_____

The assembly

- Unit of delivery and deployment
- Unit of naming for types: namespace
- Unit of security: level for granting permissions
- Unit of versioning
- Unit of side-by-side execution
- May include any number of files; "logical DLL"
- Shared or private
- Self-documenting through "manifest"

Notes:

_____

_____

_____

_____

_____

_____

Namespaces: the issue

How to resolve name conflicts between classes
    Example: CURSOR (graphics or database)
    Languages offer specific solutions:

- Packages (Ada, Java)
- Namespaces (Smalltalk, C++)
- Lace renaming (Eiffel)

Notes:

_____

_____

_____

_____

_____

_____

Namespaces in .NET

.NET provides a uniform solution through a standard hierarchical naming convention

- Example: System.Collections.Stack
- Every name fully qualified, e.g., System.Collections.Stack.pop
- Abbreviations possible in programming languages, e.g., using (C#), Lace conventions (Eiffel)

Notes:

_____

_____

_____

_____

_____

_____

Installing an assembly

- Copy the files over, including modules
- Sign the assembly using sn
- Register it using al
- Put it into the assembly cache

Notes:

_____

_____

_____

_____

_____

_____

Versioning in .NET

- Done at the assembly level
- Two kinds of assemblies: private and shared
- Versioning for shared assemblies only

Notes:

_____

_____

_____

_____

_____

_____

Runtime use of versioning information

Use only compatibility number: major.minor.build.revision

- Major and minor are the incompatible part
- Build is "possibly compatible", e.g., service pack
- Revision is "quick fix engineering" (QFE) number

Notes:

_____

_____

_____

_____

_____

Specifying which version to use

- "Only this very version", e.g., 5.0.2.7
- Latest build.revision
- "Last known good version"

Notes:

_____

_____

_____

_____

_____

An application configuration file (.cfg file)

```
<BindingPolicy>
  <BindingRedir
     Name= "ISEEiffel"
Originator="21cd4ab66e0b65a1"
     Version="*" VersionNew= "5.2.1.1"
UseLatestBuildRevision="yes"/>
  </BindingPolicy>
```

Notes:

_____

_____

_____

_____

_____

_____

Versioning

- Enables side-by-side operation of multiple versions of an application
- Applies to the .NET framework itself
- Applies within a single process
- On-the-fly replacement
- Assembly is self-contained, not just self-describing
- "Zero-impact install": FTP, XCOPY . . .
- Application isolation

Notes:

_____

_____

_____

_____

_____

_____

Assemblies and security

Security in .NET follows from a combination of techniques:

- Strongly typed code (verifiability)
- Verification of code identity by the class loader:
  - Hash signatures
  - Encrypted signatures (128-bit crypto)
- Resource permissions
  - Examples: fileIO with read, file IO with read and write, DNS access, reflection, socket, Web, registry, UI . . .
  - All assemblies in call chain must have permission ("stack walk"); cf. "ILoveYou".
- Role-based permissions

Notes:

_____

_____

_____

_____

_____

_____

Metadata

- Information associated with .NET components
- Generated by compilers
- Stored with code in executable file (.dll or .exe)

Convertible to:

- XML
- COM type libraries

Notes:

_____

_____

_____

_____

_____

_____

Execution model

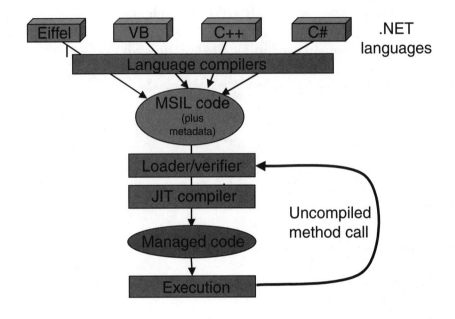

Notes:

_____

_____

_____

_____

_____

_____

The self-documentation principle

> ## Documentation is something
> ## that computers do

- Example: Eiffel "contract form"
- Reconstruct interface from code
- Tools will produce views of the system in various forms and at various levels of abstraction

Notes:

_____

_____

_____

_____

_____

Metadata contents

- Manifest: assembly description
  - Name, version, culture
  - Security properties: Needed permissions
  - Public key if present
  - Dependencies on other assemblies
- Exported and other types
  - Names
  - Interfaces implemented
  - Members: methods, fields, properties, events
- Custom attributes

Notes:

_____

_____

_____

_____

_____

_____

Examining an assembly with ildasm

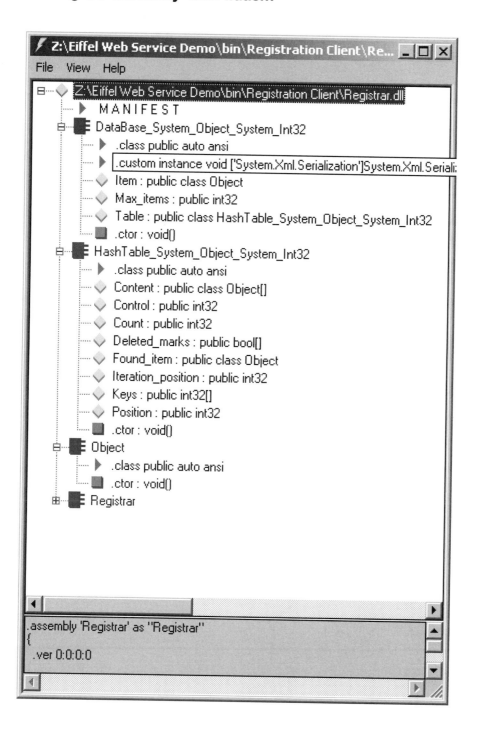

Examining IL assembler

```
╔═ Registrar::Add_registrant : void(class System.String,class System.String,class System.String,class S... ═ _ □ X ═╗

    // Code size       64 (0x40)
    .maxstack  5
    .locals (class System.Object[] V_0)
    IL_0000:  ldarg.0
    IL_0001:  ldstr       "Add_registrant"
    IL_0006:  ldc.i4.s    9
    IL_0008:  newarr      ['mscorlib']System.Object
    IL_000d:  stloc.0
    IL_000e:  ldloc.0
    IL_000f:  ldc.i4.0
    IL_0010:  ldarg.1
    IL_0011:  stelem.ref
    IL_0012:  ldloc.0
    IL_0013:  ldc.i4.1
    IL_0014:  ldarg.2
    IL_0015:  stelem.ref
    IL_0016:  ldloc.0
    IL_0017:  ldc.i4.2
    IL_0018:  ldarg.3
    IL_0019:  stelem.ref
    IL_001a:  ldloc.0
    IL_001b:  ldc.i4.3
    IL_001c:  ldarg.s     company_name
    IL_001e:  stelem.ref
    IL_001f:  ldloc.0
    IL_0020:  ldc.i4.4
    IL_0021:  ldarg.s     address
    IL_0023:  stelem.ref
    IL_0024:  ldloc.0
    IL_0025:  ldc.i4.5
    IL_0026:  ldarg.s     city
    IL_0028:  stelem.ref
    IL_0029:  ldloc.0
    IL_002a:  ldc.i4.6
    IL_002b:  ldarg.s     state
    IL_002d:  stelem.ref
    IL_002e:  ldloc.0
    IL_002f:  ldc.i4.7
    IL_0030:  ldarg.s     zip
    IL_0032:  stelem.ref
    IL_0033:  ldloc.0
    IL_0034:  ldc.i4.8
    IL_0035:  ldarg.s     country
    IL_0037:  stelem.ref
    IL_0038:  ldloc.0
    IL_0039:  call        instance class System.Object[] ['System.Web.Services']S

    IL_003e:  pop
    IL_003f:  ret
```

A source class (in Eiffel Explorer)

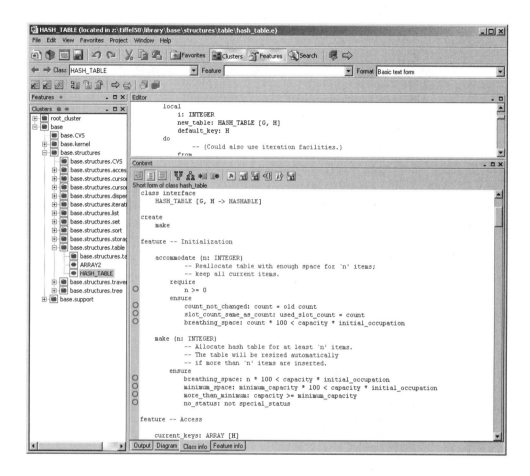

The class in ildasm

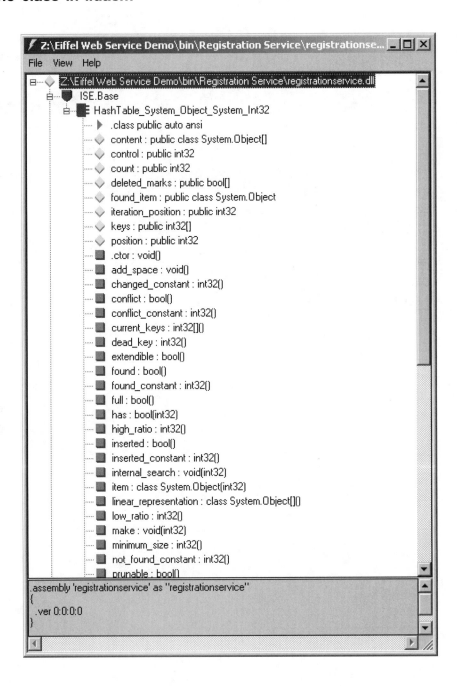

Source vs. object?

- Powerful disassembler
- Includes not only the code but the full object structure
- Has all necessary info about assembly, including dependencies
- What is a "binary component"?

Notes:

_____

_____

_____

_____

_____

_____

Custom attributes

Example: adding info (C#)

- **Using the attribute**
  ```
  [Author("Bertrand Meyer")] class MY_CLASS{...}
  ```
- **Attribute definition:**
  ```
  [AttributeUsage
      (AttributeTargets.Class|AttributeTargets.Struct)]
      public class Author : System.Attribute
          {string name;
           public Author(string n) {this.name = n}
          }
  ```

Notes:

_____

_____

_____

_____

_____

_____

Custom attributes: an example

The .NET contract wizard (ISE/Monash)

- Add contracts (preconditions, postconditions, invariants) to an existing class
- Wizard presents you with methods in turn, lets you add the various contract clauses

Notes:

_____

_____

_____

_____

_____

_____

```
class MY_WEB_PAGE inherit
      GENERIC_WEB_PAGE
feature
   refresh is
          -- Refresh the page
       require
          valid_connection: connection.open
       do
          if changed then update end
       ensure
          refreshed: old changed implies updated
       end
   ...
    changed: BOOLEAN
 invariant
    valid_connection: connection/=Void
end -- class MY_WEB_PAGE
```

Precondition

Postcondition

Class invariant

Notes:

_____

_____

_____

_____

_____

_____

Execution model

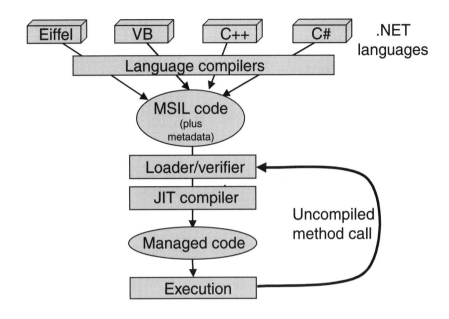

Notes:

_____

_____

_____

_____

_____

_____

JIT compilers

Two Jitters are delivered:

- Optimizing JIT
  - Global optimizations
  - Initialization may take longer
- EconoJIT
  - No global optimization
  - Faster startup
  - Caching mechanism
  - Appropriate in particular for small-footprint devices (Windows CE . . .)

Notes:

_____

_____

_____

_____

_____

_____

Managed code

- "First-class citizen" of .NET-land
- Managed code conforms to .NET object model
- Includes all the necessary metadata, information of location of object, exception handling tables...
- Benefits:
  - Memory management (garbage collection in particular)
  - Multithreading
  - Exception handling
  - Security
  - Debugging and profiling

Notes:

_____

_____

_____

_____

_____

_____

Managed code requirements

- Object model (see next)
- Objects must be garbage-collectable; strong requirements on type system
- Multiple inheritance from fully abstract classes (interfaces) only
- An example: managed vs. unmanaged C++

Notes:

_____

_____

_____

_____

_____

_____

Managed data

- Objects that can be managed by the garbage collector
- Created by programs that use references in a disciplined (type-safe) way
- Object layout: runtime provides default policy; programmer and compiler writer may specify order, layout and packing of fields
- Interaction with unmanaged data through COM Interop and PInvoke.

Notes:

_____

_____

_____

_____

_____

_____

Garbage collection in the common language runtime

- Starts from "roots"
- Detects all unreachable objects
- Compacts memory
  - Objects may move!
- Self tuning
- Two flavors: servers, interactive use
- Applies "finalization" method

Notes:

_____

_____

_____

_____

_____

_____

.NET ↔ COM interoperability: COM Interop

- Set of mechanisms to enable transition from COM to .NET, and reuse of existing COM investment
- Exposing .NET assemblies to COM:
  - Use regasm
  - To generate a type library, use tlbexp
  - Registry information automatically generated
  - To generate IDL, use OleView
- The other way around: to reuse COM components from .NET
  - Generate a "Runtime Callable Wrapper" (RCW) using tlbimp
  - Many data types automatically marshalled
  - For late-bound objects, use reflection mechanisms through System.Reflection

Notes:

_____

_____

_____

_____

_____

_____

.NET ↔ Native code interoperability

- Use PInvoke
- Takes care of finding the right function
- Takes care of transforming unmanaged values into managed objects
- Global functions only, not DLL methods

Notes:

_____

_____

_____

_____

_____

_____

Serialization

- Writes objects to persistent storage
- Automatically handled by .NET framework
- Four types:
  - Dataset (for ADO+)
  - XML
  - Binary
  - ActiveX

Notes:

_____

_____

_____

_____

_____

_____

A first comparison with the JVM

- Not meant for interpretation
- Multi-language
- Metadata goes beyond Java's reflection

Notes:

_____

_____

_____

_____

_____

_____

Lecture 11

The object model

The object model (VOS)

Type system and set of rules defining the common basis for execution in the .NET framework

Notes:

_____

_____

_____

_____

_____

_____

The basic object model

- At the centerpiece of .NET: the type system, VOS (Virtual Object System)
- Object-oriented principles: type, interface, inheritance
- Supplementary requirement for language interoperability: CLS (Common Language Specification)

Notes:

_____

_____

_____

_____

_____

_____

Strong typing

- Every value has a type
- Every reference is typed (not C/C++ model)
- All access to objects is through official features (data and function members)
- Polymorphism is controlled by inheritance

Notes:

_____

_____

_____

_____

_____

The type system

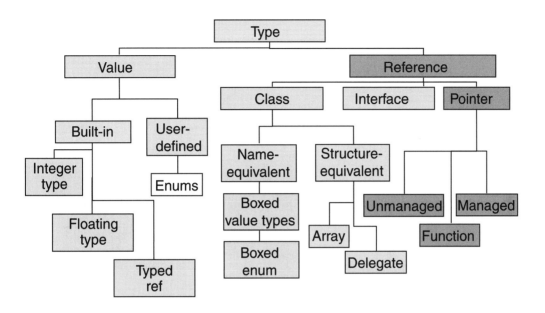

Notes:

_____

_____

_____

_____

_____

_____

Value vs. reference types

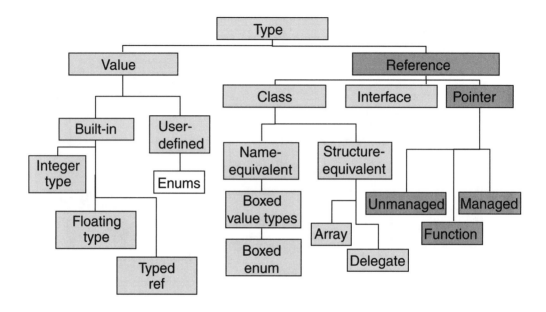

Notes:

_____

_____

_____

_____

_____

_____

Value vs. reference types

- Value types denote values (simple value or object)
- Reference type denote locations of values

Notes:

_____

_____

_____

_____

_____

_____

Difference between objects and simple values

- An object carries its own type description.
- A simple value, such as an integer, cannot by itself indicate its type. Examples: int32, float32.

Notes:

_____

_____

_____

_____

_____

_____

Objects and values

A value

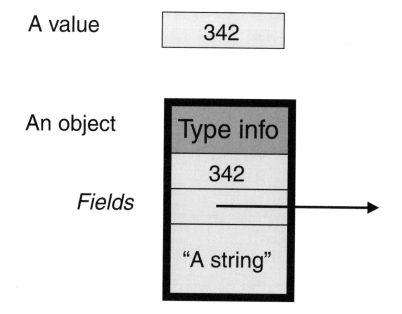

An object

Fields

Notes:

_____

_____

_____

_____

_____

Boxing and unboxing

- For every value type, there is a corresponding reference type, its boxed version.
- Boxed types have an unboxed version.
- Not all reference types can be unboxed.
- Limitation: inheritance and interfaces apply only to reference types. (See Eiffel's expanded types.)

Notes:

_____

_____

_____

_____

_____

_____

Boxing a value

A value   342

Boxed   Type info
            342

Notes:

_____

_____

_____

_____

_____

_____

Boxing and unboxing in Eiffel

- Completely general:
  - class PERSON
  - expanded class WHEEL
  - expanded class E_PERSON inherit PERSON
  - class R_WHEEL inherit WHEEL
  - x: expanded PERSON
  - y: reference WHEEL—Not yet supported

Notes:

_____

_____

_____

_____

_____

_____

Identity and equality

- Both reflexive, symmetric, transitive
  (a = a, a = b implies b = a, a = b and b = c implies a = c)
- Identity implies equality
- For identity, types must be identical, and references (for a reference type) or values (for a value type) must be identical

Notes:

_____

_____

_____

_____

_____

_____

Equality vs. identity

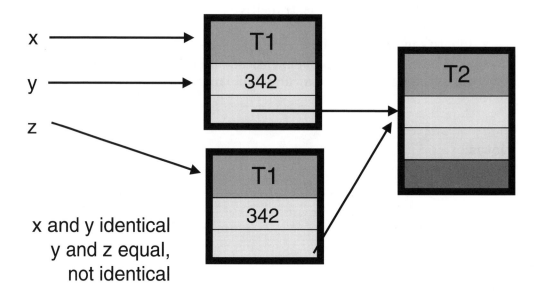

x and y identical
y and z equal,
not identical

Notes:

_____

_____

_____

_____

_____

_____

Built-in types

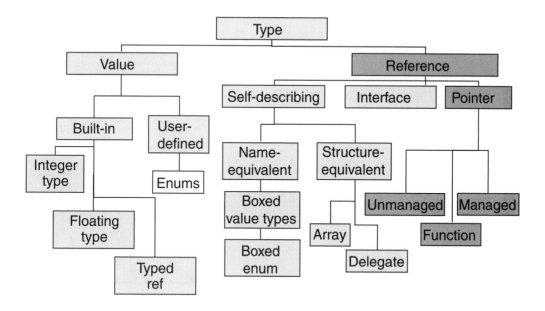

Notes:

_____

_____

_____

_____

_____

_____

Built-in types

- bool
- char
- *int8*, int16, int32, int64
- unsigned int8, *unsigned int16, unsigned int32, unsigned int64*
- *native int, native unsigned int*
- float32, float64
- System.object, System.string
- *typedref*

not in CLS

Notes:

_____

_____

_____

_____

_____

_____

Objects

- An object is an instance of a type
- An object (other than an array) is made of a number of sub-values, each described by a field of the corresponding type
- Arrays and fields are typed
- Algorithms applicable to the instances of a type are called methods

Notes:

_____

_____

_____

_____

_____

_____

Array types

- Any number of dimensions
- Arrays are objects (see class System.Array)
- (CLS) Zero lower bounds

Notes:

_____

_____

_____

_____

_____

_____

Classes in .NET

A class consists of members:

- Fields
- Methods
- Properties
- Events

Notes:

_____

_____

_____

_____

_____

_____

Possible member status

- Public
- Private
- Family (cf. "protected" in C++): descendant types only
- Assembly
- Family and assembly
- Family or assembly

Notes:

_____

_____

_____

_____

_____

_____

Properties: setters and getters

```
public class PERSON
  {private int age_internal;
   public int age
     {
     get {return age_internal}
     set {
          if (age < 0)
                {throw new Argument_exception
                    ("Negative age")
                }
          age_internal = value
     }
  }
```

Notes:

_____

_____

_____

_____

_____

_____

Information hiding violations (e.g., C++, Java)

- Direct field modification:
  ```
  x.some_field := some_value
  ```
- O-O form:
  ```
  x.set_field (some_value)

      set_field (v: TYPE) is
          do
                  field := v
          end
  ```

Notes:

_____

_____

_____

_____

_____

_____

Methods

- Algorithms associated with the class. Work on an instance, unless static.
- Instance calls or virtual calls.
- A virtual method may be overridden in a descendant class.
- A virtual method may be marked final.

Notes:

_____

_____

_____

_____

_____

Events and delegates

- Purpose: event-driven programming, e.g., GUI
- A delegate is an object representing a method of a particular class (like function pointer, but typed)
- Basic methods on delegates are Invoke, BeginInvoke, EndInvoke
- Associate one or more delegates with each event
- No way to specify "open" arguments

Notes:

_____

_____

_____

_____

_____

_____

Setting an event handler (C#, using Win Forms)

```
clickme = new Button();
clickme.Text = "Click me!";
clickme.Location = new System.Drawing.Point (200, 30);
clickme.Size = new System.Drawing.Size (65, 65);

EventHandler my_handler = new EventHandler (action);
clickme.Click += my_handler;
```

Notes:

_____

_____

_____

_____

_____

_____

The event definition

```
public class Button
  {
  public event EventHandler Click;

    protected void OnClick (EventArgs e) {
               if (Click != null) Click (this, e);
               }
  }
```

Notes:

_____

_____

_____

_____

_____

_____

Exception handling

- Uses the C++/Java model:
  ```
  try
    {code that may cause an exception}
  catch (Exception_type exc)
    {if can_fix then {fix_it}
     else throw}
  catch (Other_exception_type exc)
    {…}
  ```
- Exceptions cross language boundaries

Notes:

_____

_____

_____

_____

_____

_____

The inheritance model

- A class may extend another
- It may override some of its virtual methods
- Variables may be polymorphic
- Virtual calls on polymorphic calls will use overridden version (dynamic binding)
- Single inheritance from classes
- Multiple inheritance from interfaces

Notes:

_____

_____

_____

_____

_____

_____

Conversions

- Widening, e.g., interpret triangle as polygon: always works, e.g., p := t
- Narrowing, e.g., interpret polygon as triangle: requires runtime test (Eiffel: assignment attempt, t ?= p)
- Casts: perform actual conversions, e.g., integer to double

Notes:

_____

_____

_____

_____

_____

_____

Interfaces

- An interface is a class with no fields, and whose methods are not implemented ("abstract", "deferred")
- Descendants of the interface will add fields and implement methods
- This works with polymorphism

Notes:

_____

_____

_____

_____

_____

_____

Interfaces: the limitations

- It is often useful to have a mix of abstract and concrete ("effective") features
- Eiffel "deferred" classes permit this
- Not possible in Java and in the VOS
- Java experience shows that programmers resort to various ugly tricks to simulate this . . . (See John Viega, TOOLS USA 2000.)

Notes:

_____

_____

_____

_____

_____

_____

Multiple inheritance

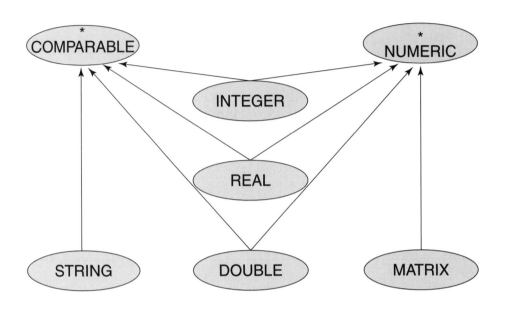

Notes:

_____

_____

_____

_____

_____

_____

deferred class COMPARABLE [G] **feature**

```
infix "<" (other: COMPARABLE [G]): BOOLEAN is
      deferred
      end
```

```
infix "<=" (other: COMPARABLE [G]): BOOLEAN is
      do
            Result:=Current < other or
                  equal (Current, other)
      end
```

```
infix ">=" (other: COMPARABLE [G]) is ...
infix ">" (other: COMPARABLE [G]) is ...
...
```
end -- class COMPARABLE

Notes:

_____

_____

_____

_____

_____

_____

The covariance issue

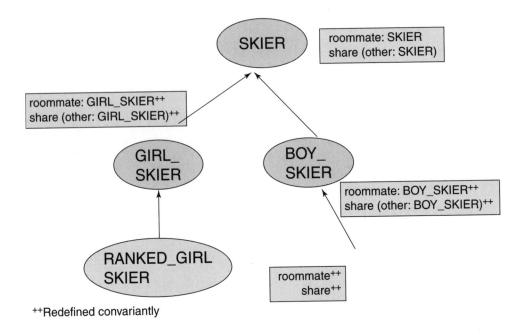

++Redefined convariantly

Notes:

_____

_____

_____

_____

_____

Covariance problems

```
b: BOY_SKIER; g: GIRL_SKIER; s: SKIER
...

s := g

s.share (b)
```

Notes:

_____

_____

_____

_____

_____

_____

The significance of covariance

- Software engineering issue
- Security issue: the O-O equivalent of buffer overflow

Notes:

_____

_____

_____

_____

_____

_____

Covariance solutions

- Static checks (not well understood)
- Dynamic checks (costly)
- Novariance (C++, Java, .NET)

Notes:

_____

_____

_____

_____

_____

_____

Covariance in .NET

- Arrays are covariant
- Other cases are not

Notes:

_____

_____

_____

_____

_____

_____

More differences with Java

- Simple values are full part of type system
- Setters and getters
- Delegates

Notes:

_____

_____

_____

_____

_____

_____

The C# language

- "Simplified version of C++"
- Benefits from the Java experience
- The native language of the .NET framework

Notes:

_____

_____

_____

_____

_____

_____

Hello world in C#

```
using System;
class Hello
  { static void Main()
  {Console.WriteLine("Hello, Dotnet"); }
  }
```

Notes:

_____

_____

_____

_____

_____

_____

C# features

- Every piece of software is in a class
- Type-safe
- Variables initialized automatically
- Versionable
- Directly interfaces with other .NET languages
- Exception handling
- Setters/getters for properties

Notes:

_____

_____

_____

_____

_____

A serious Java competitor

- Sufficiently close not to scare
- Sufficiently different to bring perceptible advantages
- Directly tied to the .NET platform

Notes:

_____

_____

_____

_____

_____

_____

Lecture 12

Language interoperability and the CLS

Language interoperability, the Java view . . .

Scott McNealy (Sun), 1997:

"Think Java. Write new applications in Java. Rewrite legacy apps with Java. Don't upgrade or downgrade. Sidegrade instead to a Java desktop device . . . I don't understand why anybody would be programming in anything other than Java."

Notes:

_____

_____

_____

_____

_____

_____

Language interoperability

- No one language suffices
- Legacy languages: COBOL, Fortran . . .
- C, C++
- Java
- Scripting languages: Python, Perl, . . .
- Ada, Eiffel
- Research languages

Notes:

Language interoperability before .NET

- Call-out and call-in
- Native Methods Interface (Java), Cecil (Eiffel)
- Limitations:
  - No cross-language inheritance: client only
  - No cross-language debugging
  - Cross-language exceptions (sometimes . . .)
  - Subtle (or not-so-subtle) type incompatibilities

Notes:

_____

_____

_____

_____

_____

_____

Languages ported or being ported to .NET

- "Microsoft languages":
  - Visual Basic
  - C#
  - C++
  - Jscript
- Commercial languages (see next)
- Research languages (see next)
- Commercial offerings from 3rd parties:
  - COBOL (Fujitsu)
  - Eiffel (ISE)
  - Smalltalk (QKS)
  - Java (Rational)
  - Perl, Python (ActiveState)
  - APL
- Research languages:
  - CAML (INRIA)
  - Mercury (Melbourne Uni.)
  - Scheme
  - Oberon (Eidgenössiche Technische Hochschule, Zürich)
  - Component Pascal (QUT)
  - Haskell (Universities, Microsoft Research UK)

Notes:

_____

_____

_____

_____

_____

Fujitsu COBOL with C# (source: B. Kadhim, Fujitsu)

Demo.cs:

```
using System;

public class Demo
{
    public static void Main ()
        {
            COBOLClass DerivedObject = new COBOLClass();
            CSharpClass BaseReference = DerivedObject;
            Console.WriteLine (BaseReference.Factorial (4));
            Console.WriteLine ("Done!");
        }
}
```

CSharpClass.cs:

```
public class CSharpClass
{
    public virtual int Factorial (int x)
    {
        int value = 0;
        for (int i = 1; i <=x; ++i)
            value = value + i;
        return value;
    }
}
```

Fujitsu COBOL with C# (source: B. Kadhim, Fujitsu) *(cont.)*

COBOL Class.cob:

```
CLASS-ID. COBOLClass INHERITS CSharpClass.
ENVIRONMENT DIVISION.
CONFIGURATION SECTION.
REPOSITORY.
    CLASS CSharpClass.
OBJECT.
PROCEDURE DIVISION.
METHOD-ID. Factorial OVERRIDE.
DATA DIVISION.
WORKING-STORAGE SECTION.
77 COUNTER PIC S9(9) COMP-5.
LINKAGE SECTION.
77 OPERAND PIC S9(9) COMP-5.
77 RETURN-VAL PIC S98(9) COMP-5.
PROCEDURE DIVISION USING BY VALUE OPERAND RETURNING RETURN-VAL.
    MOVE 1 TO RETURN-VAL.
    PERFORM VARYING COUNTER FROM 1 BY 1 UNTIL COUNTER > OPERAND
        COMPUTE RETURN-VAL = RETURN-VAL * COUNTER
    END-PERFORM.
END METHOD Factorial.
END OBJECT.
END CLASS COBOLClass.
```

Notes:

_____

_____

_____

_____

_____

Full interoperability

- Classes can inherit from each other, regardless of language of origin
- No need to write wrappers (let alone IDL)
- Cross-language debugging sessions (in Visual Studio.Net)
- Cross-language exceptions

Notes:

_____

_____

_____

_____

_____

_____

Full interoperability: the price to pay

- Must conform to VOS object model
  - May be too much for some (non-O-O languages)
  - Difficult features: overloading
  - Too little for some: multiple inheritance (Eiffel)
- Must observe CLS (see next)

Notes:

The Common Language System (CLS)

- Set of rules, more restrictive than VOS, to determine compatibility
- Three levels:
  - Producer ("framework")
  - Consumer
  - Extender

Notes:

_____

_____

_____

_____

_____

_____

Built-in types and the CLS

- bool
- char
- *int8*, int16, int32, int64
- unsigned int8, *unsigned int16, unsigned int32, unsigned int64*
- *native int, native unsigned int*
- float32, float64
- System.object, System.string
- *typedref*

not in CLS

Notes:

_____

_____

_____

_____

_____

CLS rule example

"The visibility and accessibility of types involved in a member must be at least as broad as that of the member itself"

my_routine (x: T; y: U)

- Producer: must observe this rule in exposed types and their members
- Consumer: need not accept types whose members violate this rule
- Extender: need not provide syntax to violate this rule

Notes:

_____

_____

_____

_____

_____

Example of problem rule

"An object constructor must call a base class constructor before any access occurs to inherited instance data"

- Consumer: must provide syntax for this
- Extender: must provide syntax for defining constructor methods with different signatures

(Overloading) Methods and events that have the same name must be distinguished by at least one *argument* type

- Producer: Must mark any offending methods/events as non-CLS-compliant
- Consumer: need not accept types that violate these rules, except if marked non-compliant
- Extender: need not provide syntax for defining types that violate this rule

Notes:

_____

_____

_____

_____

_____

_____

Overloading: Eiffel solution

Apply disambiguation algorithm

.NET:

```
public static void WriteLine
          (String format, Object arg0);
public static void WriteLine (int value);
public static void WriteLine (String value);
```

Eiffel:

```
WriteLine_System_String_System_Object
              (format: STRING; arg0: ANY)
WriteLine_System_Int32 (value: INTEGER)
WriteLine_System_String (value: STRING)
```

Notes:

_____

_____

_____

_____

_____

_____

Two language examples

- C++ on .NET
- Eiffel on .NET

Notes:

_____

_____

_____

_____

_____

_____

C++ on the .NET framework

Current state: two versions

- Managed
- Unmanaged

Notes:

_____

_____

_____

_____

_____

_____

Managed C++

Managed classes:

- Can inherit from any number of managed interfaces, or a managed class, or any number of managed interfaces and a managed class
- Can contain properties
- Any number of constructors, one destructor
- Can have pointers to unmanaged classes as data members
- No inheritance between managed and unmanaged
- Restrictions on cast (conversion) operations

Notes:

_____

_____

_____

_____

_____

_____

Eiffel on .NET: the good news

- Clean, simple language
- Object-oriented model, GC
- ISE implementation (Melting Ice Technology™)—already uses virtual machine
- Open environment: Interfaces with C, C++, Java™, CORBA, etc.

Notes:

_____

_____

_____

_____

_____

Eiffel on .NET: the challenges

- Genericity (parameterized classes)
- Multiple inheritance
- All-encompassing Common Language Specification:
  - Overloading, enumerated types . . .
- Support for EiffelBase and other libraries: Arrays, strings . . .
- Integration with Visual Studio .NET

Notes:

_____

_____

_____

_____

_____

_____

Eiffel on .NET: the strategy

- Initially: Support for Eiffel subset (Eiffel#)
- By 2001: Full Eiffel
- Fully integrated with rest of ISE Eiffel environment:
  - Melting Ice Technology for quick compilation
  - Browsing, debugging . . .

Notes:

_____

_____

_____

_____

_____

_____

The Eiffel# language

Subset of Eiffel mapped to the VOS

- Eiffel# includes:
  - Major language mechanisms
  - Contracts and exception handling
  - Genericity
  - Basic library
- Eiffel# does not include:
  - Multiple inheritance
  - Eiffel Agents (closures, cf. delegates)

Notes:

_____

_____

_____

_____

_____

_____

Toward a common development environment

- Visual Studio.NET (mid-2001?)
- Common API
- Common back end, editing, browsing, debugging tools
- Currently: Microsoft languages

Notes:

_____

_____

_____

_____

_____

_____

PART E

ASSESSMENT AND

PERSPECTIVE

 Lecture 13: The future of .NET

Lecture 13

The future of .NET

Problems addressed

- Single model for Web and non-Web (e.g., client-server) development
- Web services
- Easy deployment of applications
- Application versioning
- Application security
- Application independence
- Dealing with many languages
- Component combination with lean interfaces

Notes:

_____

_____

_____

_____

_____

_____

Some immediate practical consequences

- End of "DLL Hell"
- "Smart Web sites"
- Multi-language development, including multi-language inheritance, debugging . . .
- No more IDL
- Strong security mechanisms
- Standard database interface: ADO+
- Scalability: from PDA to Web farm

Notes:

_____

_____

_____

_____

_____

.NET opens up the game

- Several languages
- Robust, scalable solutions
- No more dilemma between performance and interoperability
- Integrates the Web seamlessly into traditional computing (and conversely)
- Powerful, coherent object model

Notes:

_____

_____

_____

_____

_____

_____

A few lessons

- Java is no longer the only game in town
- The first nail in the C++ coffin
- Components are the same things as objects
- The revenge and triumph of object technology

Notes:

_____

_____

_____

_____

_____

How to prepare

- Explore demos (e.g., dotnet.eiffel.com)
- Explore relationship between Web and rest of IT
- Explore ASP+
- Study the type system
- Study betas as they converge towards product
- Clean up C++ applications
- Consider other languages

Notes:

_____

_____

_____

_____

_____

_____